In *Living Life on Purpose*, Katie Ashley provides a roadmap for readers to engage with one of life's most important questions: How can I feel happy no matter my experience? Katie shows you how to work through your biggest challenges to be the one guiding your soul's ship. There is a central message throughout her book that says: You are already whole.

Living Life on Purpose is a modern day "click your heels three times, Dorothy." When you finish reading, you'll realize you had the power to actualize your life all along. You just needed the tools to see more clearly.
— **Manorama**
Founder, The Sanskrit Studies Method
Founder, The Luminous Soul Method

With wit and wisdom, Katie Ashley shares from the heart in such a way that *Living Life on Purpose* feels like a conversation with a trusted friend. If you enjoy exploring fresh ways to live consciously and with deep intention, you won't be disappointed!
— **Melanie Klein, Sociology & Women's Studies Professor,**
Yoga & Body Image co-editor and co-founder of the Yoga
and Body Image Coalition

Katie has written the book she wished she had while struggling with her own body issues. Another great addition to the field - she tells us that it can be different if we find our authentic selves. A lesson that we all need to hear.
— **Brandt Passalacqua, yoga therapist, Peaceful Weight Loss**

Living Life on Purpose weaves together a fabric of past experience and light-hearted wisdom. Katie uses humor as she accurately introduces yogic philosophy and personal accounts to explain how life can be lived with purpose, on purpose, for a vibrantly meaningful existence over the long haul.

If you're wondering if you have no option but to allow the decisions of your past to map out your future, read this book and rewrite the end to your story.
— **Caryn Antos O'Hara, Ayurvedic Specialist,**
Yoga Instructor, Survivor

Living Life on Purpose makes the abstract practical and the practical liveable with this insightful sharing of one aspirant journey.
— **Jules Febre, International Yoga Teacher**

Living Life On Purpose

Living Life On Purpose

A collection of essays, stories, and timeless teachings from a modern perspective

KATIE ASHLEY

ISBN-13: 9781517492779
ISBN-10: 1517492777

Foreword

We're all born into a helpless and ignorant state of being. We are born craving love, attention, safety, nourishment, and belonging. We develop our sense of self based on the environment we're raised in — our home life, school life, social life, and culture.

Although it may be possible that we're born with some karmic momentum from previous incarnations, for the most part, I believe our personalities, behavior patterns, and self-esteem are the product of our upbringing. It's by no fault or intention of our own that we feel how we feel and act how we act in this life. The human condition is further compounded by an ancient evolutionary biological survival instinct that doesn't stop craving stimulation and gratification from the external, even when we get what we need. We are driven by the desire for pleasure, aversion to all things unpleasant, and a self-centered tendency to take it all very personal.

At some point in life (and sometimes in a life or death crisis), we become aware of our personality, habitual patterns, and the identity that's been imposed upon us. We see that without intentional actions, we are truly just the product of our environment. We don't have all that much choice in how we turn out. But with intention and purpose, we have the ability to see clearly and respond wisely to all that has and will transpire in this lifetime.

Katie has offered us a wonderful map to some of the transformational practices and investigations that have the potential, when applied diligently, to allow us to live the life we desire, rather than the one we inherited. Through her personal stories, honest struggles, and clear insight, she guides us toward an authentic life, one that is meaningful and wise.

May you benefit from these teachings. May you become a refuge unto yourself and others. Together may we create a positive change on this planet.

Noah Levine

Refuge Recovery, Heart of the Revolution, Against the Stream, Dharma Punx

Conceptual and primary editing by Alison Sher of Epilogue Editorial
+ Design
Cover photo by Anna Ward of Anna Ward Photography

To those who are ready to stand up, break free, and live on purpose.

Table of Contents

How To Use This Book

It seems like whenever I pick up a spiritual text, I open the page and read exactly what I need to guide me along my path. The books that create the most radical shifts in our lives can be read again and again because our understanding of the wisdom on each page changes as we do. When we reread our favorite passage — in a few moments, the next day, or after many years — the words have a different meaning because we've grown. There are multiple ways to apply wisdom to our lives. When we feel connected to a book, its lessons evolve with us.

This collection of essays and stories is filled with ancient teachings shared through my modern perspective. Each chapter is a little piece of my heart, a personal story married with the teachings of yoga and Buddhism that have taught me to stand up and break free in my life.

My hope is that *Living Life on Purpose* will help you know yourself a bit better, and perhaps, start living your life in a new way. When we live our lives on purpose, we take flight while rooting. Living on purpose is like dancing to rock and roll in a cloud of glitter or walking barefoot through the grass while carrying a warm mug of tea. That's what it feels like to me.

At the end of each chapter is space for you to record your thoughts. Make this book your own. Keep a pen nearby. Read a chapter. Tune into yourself. Take a deep breath and then let go. Write down whatever comes up. Don't edit your thoughts. Let the words flow from your heart to the page.

The lessons in these essays are designed to build on each other. They can also be read in any order. If you need help understanding any italicized spiritual terms, go to the index to find their meaning.

And one last note: as always, question all teachings. Hold them to the mirror of your life. What does your experience confirm to be true? You must be willing to watch your world shift as you use the teachings to look at life from a different perspective.

There is a Sanskrit *mantra,* Lokah Samastah Sukhino Bhavantu.

It means may all beings everywhere be happy and free, and may the thoughts, words, and actions of my own life contribute in some way to that happiness and to that freedom for all.

I've realized (after a lot of trial and error) that to be at peace, and to be of service to others, I must live my life on purpose.

Svaha. May it be so.

Much love,
Katie Ashley
www.katieashley.org

Standing At The Precipice

Lessons on Dharma

*T*he *Bhagavad Gita* is a 700-verse Hindu scripture found within the ancient text of the *Mahabharata*. In it, we are told the epic story of *Arjuna*. He stands beside *Krishna*, his guide and charioteer. They are on a steep cliff overlooking *Dharma Yuddha*, a righteous war that Arjuna is meant to fight. Arjuna represents the human soul seated in the chariot of the body. Krishna is the inner Spirit, the God within, who is there for counsel.

Arjuna is struggling. He's supposed to join the war, but to do so would be to harm and kill friends and family fighting on the other side. Krisha offers Arjuna a teaching on *dharma* — the law and order of the universe that, when channeled, can help a person realize their true cosmic nature. He explains that it's Arjuna's dharma to fight. That's why he's a warrior. He must fight to fulfill his dharma and, in doing so, attain liberation.

The problem of war has been around forever. Today, humanity is still divided against itself, threatened with mutually assured destruction. No political means have proven themselves adequate to deal with this problem, leaving many people destroyed by violence, living in despair. The *Gita* teaches that it is only when we rise above human schemes and calculations that we awaken to the presence of our spirit and fulfill our need for peace. We transcend the dangers of a dualistic world at war.

This is the goal of *yoga* — to join with the Divine, which we learn is within each of us. We can do this through a practice of yoga and meditation, studying the ancient texts, and reciting mantras and prayers. However, it's often most effective to find teachers who have mastered enough of their own ego that they can help us clearly see the cause and effect of what we do. They can steer us to become more peaceful. They can witness us without judgment as we emotionally process our experiences. They can help us understand our human conditioning so we can return to the Divine.

The topic of the teacher can be a sticky one. In the West, people tend to be skeptical about the relationship between a student and a *guru* because of secularism, stories of exploitative student-teacher power plays, the fear of handing one's will over to another person, and the disbelief that anyone could ever be a "perfect" human. I've greatly benefited from both studying with my beloved teachers and from questioning them. There are people who are more conscious than others, and yet even they still have blind spots.

It doesn't have to be either or. It can be both and. We can live in paradox.

The teacher comes in many forms. Sometimes it's a person. Sometimes it's a song, an animal, a moment of celebration, or a painful realization. And sometimes the teacher is a book, like *The Gita*.

A teacher, in the form of a person, helped me step into my dharma when she gave me the direction I was struggling to give myself. At the time, I had been flying back and forth between Seattle and Charleston, piecing together my education to create my career. I had been working as a Pilates instructor after teaching dance, group fitness, and personal training for years. I had studied psychology, philosophy, and nutrition, and in Seattle, I was furthering my training in Integrative Movement Therapy for adults. A few years later, I would go on to earn certifications and continuing education in yoga, plant-based nutrition, yoga for anxiety and depression, and yoga therapy. At the time, major parts of the puzzle were still missing.

I'd dedicated myself to healing and self-exploration for the past decade — in an effort to stay alive. For much of that time, doing well meant I wasn't teetering on the edge of self-destruction or drowning myself in the chaos of an eating disorder or the dramatic and direction-less existence that I'd come to know after giving up my dance career. I decided a decade ago to do whatever it would take to become healthy and find a new path. My dreams of who I wanted to be felt very ethe-real at first, not at all like a potential reality. I knew nothing but this: I wanted to make an impact and live a life that had meaning and purpose.

Bit by bit, I rehabilitated myself as I studied and created the founda-tion for my career. I made the path up as I went along by listening to my heart and trusting my intuition, even when (especially when) it didn't make logical sense.

On my birthday, I went to one of my favorite yoga classes at my favorite studio. Whenever a student has a birthday celebration at Satsang Yoga Charleston *yoga shala*, the entire class gathers in a circle around that person and sings a lovely mantra. As I sat in the center, my teacher, Jeffrey, mentioned that I would become a *Jivamukti Yoga* teacher.

I never planned on going to teacher training. Prior to that moment, I never mentioned out loud that I was even considering it. I wouldn't let myself believe it was possible. Yet sitting in that circle with so many friends and teachers around me, I knew without a doubt that going to teacher training was important. It was the missing link in my personal life and career. I felt ready.

Everything was aligned except for one massive issue: I had no idea how I was going to pay for a $10,000 training and leave town for a month. The idea of going brought up every fear around my self-worth, my relationship with money and success, and my ability to ask for and receive help. Every day for a month, I felt like I was standing at the door of a plane flying at an altitude of 2,000 feet, knowing I had to jump. Would the parachute work if I did?

I was terrified of giving up and choosing not to go. I was terrified of declaring I would attend only to get crushed when I couldn't get the funds together. And I knew it was a turning point, although I didn't know then why or how true that statement would turn out to be.

Then my teachers' teachers — David Life and Sharon Gannon, the founders of Jivamukti Yoga — came to town. I arrived to class early and rolled out my mat in the second row on the left side of the large ballroom, directly behind Polly, my acupuncturist, dear teacher, and beloved friend.

I talked to Polly more openly and honestly about my life than anyone else. She knew all of my past and present struggles. She listened, offered acupuncture treatments and life lessons, but she never tried to "fix" anything for me. She taught me the value of having someone who stands by you and allows you to be exactly who you are, trusting the process as you grow and evolve, offering support as opposed to solutions.

At the start of class, David introduced himself and Sharon and then asked every Jivamukti-certified yoga teacher to stand up. He then asked for the people who were going to become Jivamukti teachers that year to also rise.

Immediately, I could feel myself back on that plane, unsure about the parachute. Except this time, the plane was on fire, heading straight into a mountain range. I went pale and started to shake. I was Arjuna at the precipice of battle.

Polly turned around and said, "Stand up!" And I did. I stood up in front of all of my teachers, many of my friends, and at least a hundred other people I didn't know.

The money came in the most beautiful way as the owners of Satsang Yoga, Jeffrey Cohen and Andrea Boyd, taught a fundraising class in my honor. Other movement teachers from the area came together and created a full-day event with yoga, tai chi, Nia, and Pilates. They generously donated the profits to my tuition fund. My parents offered to make a large contribution, and I miraculously was able to earn and save more money in one month than I ever had before.

Each time I received funds, I sent them straight to the Omega Institute, where the teacher training took place, and checked my remaining balance. A few days before the deadline, I still had a rather scary amount of money left to pay. I chose to call again, just to confirm the number I swore I already knew. Except this time when I inquired, the person on the phone said I'd received a scholarship and that my remaining balance was less than $200. I had enough in my checking account to make the final payment. I began teacher training a few months later on Easter Sunday.

It all started with the words "stand up."

I don't mean to physically get on your feet. I mean step into life. Claim your direction despite your fears.

Are you ready to stand up? I always ask my students this when we begin to work together. Because it's a choice — to live our dharma or spend our lives running from it. To stand up or sit down. There is no in-between. We can't play small. We can't let fear control our lives, because those fears will eventually determine our reality.

If we allow millions of excuses to consume our minds, we'll never create the lives we were born to live. When we choose to stand up, what unfolds is amazing. We commit to the journey of discovering how life can work. The experience of living starts to feel like magic. It's a meaningful, purposeful unfolding.

We realize that every move, even the steps backwards, are guiding us toward the actualization of our dharma and *moksha*, liberation. We all have a wonderful opportunity to learn about ourselves. We are liberated by making choices that bring us into alignment with spirit, by working the intelligent design of the universe that can guide us to our highest potential. When what we say and what we do match our values and our goals, we get to where we want to go.

Stand up. Choose your destiny.

Exercise #1

1.) Take a deep breath and ask yourself the following: Where in my life do I need to stand up? Why am I waiting?
Be brave and answer with your heart and intuition. The answer coming from your heart and intuition will be different than the critical thoughts that play on repeat in your mind. The quieter you can become, the easier it is to hear the voice of spirit. Give yourself the time to gain clarity.
2.) Once you have an answer, ask yourself this: In what way can I take real action to stand up today? What's the first step? Make a few notes in the space provided.

Holy Girl, Party Girl

Having Fun & Finding Answers on the Middle Path

*H*ave you ever met someone who always stays on track, follows the rules, meets deadlines, wears put-together, fashionable clothes, and colors inside the lines? Then there's the other extreme — someone who rebels and resists at every opportunity. Sometimes it's to support a cause or an ideal, and sometimes they defy rules just because. Most people seem to fall closer to one side of the spectrum than the other. I tend to ping-pong between the two.

When we deepen our study of yoga, we begin to use the philosophy to understand ourselves and the nature of life. Some teachings will restore you like deep breaths of fresh air, while others are harder to digest.

I used to find the concept of *sattva* off-putting. Sattva is one of the *gunas,* a term in Hindi that categorizes all aspects of material reality.

Sharon Gannon and David Life define the three gunas in this way:

1. Sattva: Lightness, purity, tranquility, goodness, balance.
2. Rajas: Activity, passion, growth, change, evolution.
3. Tamas: Darkness, inertia, heaviness, resistance, involution.

I thought I was supposed to be completely sattvic (sattva) at all times to be a yogi. I thought I needed to give up my raja, my rebellious, punky, playful, mischievous, late-night dance party aspects of myself to walk this path as a teacher. To do so was a massive betrayal to my nature.

This internal struggle colored much of my experience in teacher training, so much so that on graduation day, Sharon said to me, "I know that this has been really hard for you."

I didn't expect her to say those words, but in a sense, they were exactly what I needed to hear. They helped me let go of my attachment to any teacher's opinion of me. I also had to let go of thinking that we must fit into one of the guna categories perfectly and completely, for humans are far more dimensional than that. We are a beautiful mix of all three. At times, we can be sattvic, other times more rajasic. And sometimes, we are tamasic. All three have prupose in our experience of life.

I've learned a great deal in my sattvic moments. Discipline, devotion, and stillness have much to offer. So do action, adventure, and ridiculous amounts of random fun, sometimes the lesson we need comes from a place that can only be accessed by shaking stuff up.

When I am sitting at my computer feeling uninspired, I don't sit in meditation or listen to dharma talks or chant mantras. I put in my ear buds, pump up the volume, and rock out to gritty rockabilly tunes. Inspiration always strikes. I am freed from my tamastic state.

There was a time when I felt stuck in my life a few years ago. I was heartbroken but still in love. My partner (and future father of my son) and I had broken up yet again despite my deep faith in us. I was grid-locked in my work. I didn't have a plan of action to make the transition from teaching Pilates full time to making a career out of mentoring, writing, and yoga. Charleston, South Carolina, somehow had turned into my home, although I thought my time here was done.

In the past, I would have gone full steam ahead down one of two paths: either the sattvic path of seeking counsel from my teachers, meditating on my situation, praying for guidance, doing nothing while convincing myself that I had full faith God or the Universe had a bigger plan for me and that the pain and confusion were meant to teach me something. Or I would have burned my whole life down and run away — cut ties in relationships, moved to a different city, dyed my hair, bought new clothes, gone out dancing and drinking pretty much every night, deciding that nothing made sense, everything was random, and there was no divine order to anything. I knew my patterns and was determined not to fall into either extreme.

My friend and I were at the beach on a beautiful, super sunny Charleston day, having fun swimming and walking while talking about yoga, life, and love, when huge, angry, dark storm clouds rolled into the sky.

We decided to drive to the mountains. Just like that. We jumped into my Miata in our bikinis, kept the convertible top down, and raced through the rain all the way to Asheville, North Carolina. We almost blew out the stereo speakers on the way there. We didn't have anything with us except the clothes we were wearing.

We spent the night at one of my favorite places on Earth, my aunt and uncle's farm, then had a great morning in town. We ate fancy chocolate, window-shopped, wandered through art galleries and funky little shops, drank kombucha on draft, and flirted with everyone. I didn't shed all my boundaries and get wasted or go home with someone or do anything risky I'd regret. And I didn't sit and meditate and try to be superhumanly stoic, pretending my heart wasn't aching.

When we got back, my clarity was on fire. Not because I knew what path to take, but because I was okay with my not knowing. The need to make a choice on how to respond to the situation no longer felt so heavy. The trip was so fun that the wounds started healing. I could return to the mat and look to my practice for guidance again. In a sense, I had found *the middle path*.

The goal of devotional practice is to be who you are, where you are, how you are, and to love and accept it. Having the kind of fun that makes you feel 100 percent you — down to your bones — is essential.

We are not monks or nuns. We're people of this crazy world. It's tempting to keep our nose to the grindstone and relentlessly pursue self-growth as a way out of our pain. However, when we become so focused on "doing the work," we forget to enjoy the life we are so tenaciously trying to create. Sometimes the answer is to stop focusing so hard on finding answers and give ourselves space.

Think of a Magic 8 Ball. Sometimes you shake it and get the message "try again later." This can be a wise answer. Let the seeds grow and the dust settle. Sometimes a little fire creates a sense of calm. We can have faith and have fun.

Exercise #2

1.) Where do you need more joy and spontaneous fun in your life?
2.) What can you do today that would be amazingly fun for you?

Voice Lessons

Speaking Your Truth

Haunting Memory

I was at a family cookout playing hide-and-seek with a few other kids and some adults. It was my turn to hide. A man who was playing with us picked me up, hid me inside a trashcan, and then closed the lid. I was petrified, but I knew I was supposed to be quiet. I liked to follow the rules to avoid getting in trouble, so I stayed silent.

I have no idea how long I was in the trashcan or how I got out. Maybe I started crying, or maybe the game ended and the man came back to get me. I could have been in there for only been a few seconds or maybe up to 15 minutes. However long it was, being stuck and unable to use my voice has remained one of the most anxiety-inducing themes of my life.

- End Scene -

When I was in my teens and early twenties, I would often find myself in environments that I didn't want to be in and couldn't escape, because I couldn't use my voice. I forced myself to stay silent. I wouldn't speak up, because I didn't want to hurt anyone. I stayed loyal to unhealthy situations. I would shut down, act quiet and agreeable until my insides were dying. Then I would either speak up in a defensive burst of anger or squash my feelings with substances and other distracting but self-destructive behaviors. I felt the pain of large groups of society — anyone who had assumptions made about them or was marginalized due to their race, sexuality, religion, socioeconomic status, taste in music, or sense of style. I knew what it felt like to be trivialized.

Once I realized I was creating these situations for myself by choosing to stay in them, I made a commitment to respond differently. I was on a mission to find my voice and use it. I learned to leave the people that didn't respect me. And over time, I stopped finding myself trapped in cages of my own creation.

Still, sometimes in life we can't always escape every situation that makes us comfortable. We'll find ourselves stuck in difficult interactions — sandwiched in the middle seat next to a grumpy man on an international flight, at a holiday dinner with family members who have polar-opposite political views, forced to face someone who lashes out about something we shared on social media.

In the past, whenever I felt unheard, misrepresented, misunderstood, judged, demeaned, doubted, or seen as incapable, I would take it personally. People acted the way they did because there was something wrong with me. Now I know that the way people treat me is a reflection of how they treat themselves. What they say and do is a product of their deeply held personal beliefs, what their experience has confirmed, and how they've learned to protect themselves as they walk through life, although it might conflict with what I think and believe, and need to do for myself.

I used to create a massive barrier in my heart between myself and whoever attacked me. I would react instead of respond. My first impulse was to become submissive instead of approaching the experience as an opportunity to take my power back from others while learning to navigate the dynamics of the world in a more peaceful way.

I first began to flex my constructive conflict muscles bartending and waitressing at a downtown pizza place owned by two Italian brothers from New York. The restaurant was staffed with drunk and hyper college students and professional food and beverage workers full of rough edges. Working there was boot camp for learning to choose what to take to heart and what to quickly shrug off.

I had just moved to Charleston after bouncing around across the country, making very impulsive choices with good intentions and awful results. I was committed to leaving everywhere and everyone that wasn't healthy for me. I also knew I had to stop running away every time I felt challenged or when my expectations were disappointed. I needed to get lessons from each situation and gracefully evolve. I was working on discerning the best way to handle what I was creating in my life because the appropriate response was different in every scenario.

I had to realize it's okay to have a different opinion than someone else, even if the opposing party is larger, louder, and in a position of authority. I went from being timid to really enjoying my job by speaking up and building both boundaries and connections. I had to kick everyone out of the bar at last call. I had to tell other bartenders from different restaurants they weren't allowed to get free pizza and beer. I had to come up with the most right response when challenged by the owner's father about whether or not I had requested a slice of pizza be put into the oven.

Each of those examples seem like trivial points now, but at the time, they felt hugely difficult and I felt small. The truth was that I was enough. I had something to offer to our team by letting myself be who I was. We were all young and wild and working in a very strange and weirdly special place. To survive, I had to learn when it's productive to speak up and when it's not helpful, because there are things you can't change about people and the reality of a situation, so don't even try. All you can do is choose to be there with your whole heart and know when to draw the line. As a result, one of those Italian brothers became a lifelong friend.

- Scene Two -

Over ten years later, I was stuck once again, this time at a dinner table with a member of my extended family, who was lecturing me about race, poverty, and the abuse of the entitlement system. He made many judgmental and derogatory comments about society's underclass. I was highly offended and sad. The dinner conversation started out as something else. I had no idea how it went down this strange rabbit hole. I was being talked *at* from a place of extreme attachment to deep beliefs that this other person was treating as the ultimate reality. Speaking from my heart and trying to find common ground was not working. My attempts to advocate for those being disparaged fell on indignant, deaf ears.

It had been a long time since I'd experienced a situation like this. My social connections had become so expertly curated in the process of learning to declare my value. I'd created such a strong *satsang* (community) that most of the people I interacted with on a daily basis were also working on mindfulness, nonviolence, and making space to understand and respect others to deepen their connection to the whole of life. I almost always find myself in deep conversations that are not debates or lectures.

It's natural to gravitate toward affinity groups of people who are like you to avoid conflict, but we still have to live in the larger world, filled with people who are different from us. What happens then? What happens when we're smashed with someone who challenges us on every level? We can't always avoid these interactions. Yet if we close ourselves off in our comfortable bubbles, we can never truly achieve *yoga*, union, the ability to find oneness with all that is.

To find union with all that is, I must stay open. And living life wide open means I'll get hurt. I'll be disappointed. People will take advantage of my trust. It also means I'll be able to see and feel love in places others won't. I will have moments when my faith and trust in humanity is affirmed. I'll be able to see the beauty in people that I wouldn't be able to from a self-imposed cage of fear, judgment, and hate.

It seemed like this family member had shut down due to his own fears, judgements, and hatred. He was like a person who had eaten a few bad potatoes and vowed to stop eating potatoes for the rest of his life, along with every other vegetable. And he also had a point. There are people who misuse the system. Crime is rampant in impoverished areas. However, these realities caused him to harshly cast aside an entire social group, so much so that he no longer had the desire to uplift these people or cultivate compassion for their struggles. And yet I had to accept this person as he was. I needed to be able to see that he is not his opinions. I needed to see the goodness he has to offer in other ways and recognize the compassion he does have for people he can relate to.

The yoga teachings of *Patanjali* offer guidance on how to take the good with the bad without being disheartened. In the *Yoga Sutras*. Sutra I:33 says, "By cultivating attitudes of friendliness toward the happy, compassion for the unhappy, delight in the virtuous, and disregard toward the wicked, the mind-stuff retains its undisturbed calmness." (Translation by Shri Swami Satchidananda.)

This sutra teaches us the four keys:

1. *Maitri*, Friendliness.
2. *Karuna*, Compassion.
3. *Mudita*, Delight.
4. *Upekshanam,* Disregard.

These four keys unlock the four locks:

1. Happy people
2. Unhappy people
3. The virtuous
4. The wicked

When we use the proper key in the proper lock, we can retain our peace of mind in a world full of people learning how to cope with danger, confusion, betrayal, and grief. If we forget our keys, we needlessly experience anger, judgment, hate, jealousy, distrust, and a host of other uncomfortable feelings. It's important to feel our uncomfortable feelings as they arise. However, we don't need to defend them or act in ways that cause them to become stronger.

I tried my best at dinner to use the key of compassion, but eventually the key of disregard was needed. Ignoring someone doesn't mean they are wicked or evil by nature. It means you experience their words and actions as threatening or harmful, so it's best to keep your distance. In many situations, we will need to use a combination of keys to remove the locks and find the divinity within others. And a voice is always needed.

Exercise #3

1.) What people or situations are you struggling with? Write them down.
2.) How does it feel in your body to struggle with a situation of ideological conflict? What does it remind you of from your past?
3.) How can you use the four keys to unlock your struggle?
Take a moment to tune into yourself and then make a few notes in the space provided.

Beyond Halfway

Love is Your Highest Potential

I spent years completely disconnected from my body and emotions. Ironically, I was the most out of touch with my body when I was using it the most — at age 18 while studying dance and theater in college and teaching and choreographing with a dance company in the summer. On average, I danced at least six hours a day. When I wasn't dancing, I hyper-focused on food and my weight. I created beautiful binders full of carefully curated recipes printed on color-coded paper and neatly organized them on my shelf in my shared dorm room. Except I never made any of those meals, because I had an eating disorder.

Perfectionism was my escape from my vulnerability. I became obsessed with rewriting notes from class in freakishly neat handwriting. I would study for hours even if I didn't care about the subject. No matter how controlled I tried to be, I couldn't make my feelings go away. I needed everything to be perfect so desperately that it made me angry and sad if someone read the newspaper and folded the sections out of order. If I was using my intellect to organize and micromanage and memorize facts and figures, I didn't have to look at my problems or feel my feelings or face the fact I had spun far off center.

I never could have admitted it at the time, but I desperately wanted to to escape my life. I didn't want to die, but I did not want the life I was living. I wanted out of the relationship I'd been in since the end of high school. I went from being the captain of the dance team and a star studio student to an average dancer in my new company and freshman college class. I didn't want to be average. I didn't want to feel like I gave up on my dreams by going to college in Ohio instead of moving to New York City like I'd always planned. I wanted to blame others for my choices and my health instead of my own fear.

Since I couldn't erase my emotions, and I didn't think I was capable of changing my situation, I restricted myself of food and exercised compulsively. I manipulated my body to unhealthy degrees and focused on the feeling of starvation to avoid the voice inside me that was screaming in pain and desperation. It seemed to work for awhile, until the life I created put me at serious risk of dying.

After a few hospitalizations for malnutrition and dehydration, I agreed to admit myself into a residential eating disorder treatment facility in South Florida. I was so thin, my body too unstable to fly in an airplane, that my mom and I made the long drive from Ohio ourselves. When we stopped for the night in Savannah, Georgia, I asked her to take a photo of me in a swimsuit for the day I could look back at myself with a healthy perspective. I knew my current vision was extremely skewed. I knew it was time to get better. And I will never forget her expression that evening. She was so scared and sad, but at the same time proud of me for asking.

I would love to say that this realization is when I started living on purpose, but it wasn't the catalyst. I simply channeled all my compulsions and perfectionism into playing by the rules of recovery. It was a game of make-believe rather than real healing. I was gaining weight, but I still wasn't able to trust my mind or listen to my feelings. My treatment team encouraged me to forfeit my dance scholarship to college and find a new life path. I had to let go of a huge piece of my identity, pretty much the only part about myself, aside from my family, that ever felt like an extension of my heart.

I filled the void of that loss with self-destructive substances, relationships, jobs, and living arrangements. Having every resource but not knowing how to live a healthy life is a crushing dilemma. I had met plenty of people who were happy to go with the flow and let life happen, and the outcome of their actions wasn't half as disastrous as mine. I needed big passion and purpose to sustain my existence, and I couldn't find examples of it anywhere.

I was in crisis again, but of a different kind. I lost dance, and I nearly lost my family. My parents, who had always been in my corner, made a heartbreaking but wise choice and stopped enabling me with money, instead offering me the option to come back to Ohio to live with them. I knew staying dependent on them wasn't the right path. I would love to say that my knowing was due to a deep connection to my intuition, but in that moment, it was a mix of fear, stubbornness, shame, and rebellion.

I had no one to turn to for guidance, and I didn't have the tools to look within myself for answers. Out of stubbornness and defiance, I chose to stay in South Florida and try to find my friends (who were in and out of halfway homes) that I'd let live with me when my parents were paying for my apartment. When I couldn't find them, I chose to camp out underneath a lifeguard stand with no real plan of where to go from there.

I was about to take a bus to look for those "friends" (I couldn't even tell you their names now) when an old woman at the bus stop looked at me and said, "Sometimes God makes it so that we have to take another route."

There had to be a different way. In that moment, I knew there had to be a different way to live.

Luckily, South Florida is not such a bad place to be when you have nowhere to live and nothing to do. I found my way to the coffee shop I frequented when I was in extended outpatient treatment. I ran into a girl there who said she had a friend in search of a live-in part-time nanny. I was not qualified for the job but got hired. When I wouldn't sleep with my employer, I was fired.

By that time, I'd saved a little cash and created some positive relationships, including a boyfriend who was able to see in me the girl I wanted to be. I fell in love, for real, for the first time. And although I eventually ran away from the relationship, it was a corrective experience, a massive turning point.

I was on track, but I didn't flip a switch into full recovery. I relapsed once in my eating disorder after moving away from South Florida. I was more deeply aware of what I was doing to myself, but I didn't know any other way to cope with the chaos of not knowing what to do with my life, once again trying out a bunch options and hating them all. I used my eating disorder to get back into rehab to escape the life I was creating for myself.

I never chose to be anorexic, but I chose to overcome anorexia. As time passed, my crisis became largely existential. I no longer had an eating disorder or abused other kinds of substances. My problem was that I had no idea who I was. I would experiment with subcultures and odd friendships and hairdos, taking on pieces of the identity of whoever I was around, trying to find my place. Although I was unsure of a lot, each positive encounter created subtle shifts in my well-being.

It still took me a very long time to find my way into an unconditionally loving relationship with my body, thoughts, and emotions, mainly because I was still attached to the external being a certain way. It wasn't until I began to free dance in Nia and move my body in *yoga asana* that I stopped loving myself halfway and developed a sense of unconditional loyalty to the spirit within me. I slowly reprogrammed my mind and body to move through the world with increased clarity, joy, and efficacy.

Our culture often teaches us to identify exclusively with our thoughts and regard our physical body as something to change, hide, polish up, and parade around. We learn to attach massive amounts of self-esteem and self-worth to our bodies, while at the same time we identify our real self as the thoughts inside our head. We are taught to apologize for our feelings and condemn ourselves and others for expressing emotions that don't seem polite or ideal. We are taught to hate and ignore everything that makes us real.

To truly feel our feelings is terrifying to most of us because if we did, we'd have to change our lives, relationships, and the way we communicate. If we felt our feelings, we'd start to feel the impact of the decisions we've made and the blows others have given us. It seems easier to avoid them by drowning our sadness, anger, and fear in alcohol, pushing them away with food, getting a hit of dopamine by picking up a random person at the bar, spending money we don't have, or zoning out in a Netflix binge. There is far more messaging encouraging us to seek quick escapes than there are sources that offer us the wisdom needed to teach us how to embrace this messy, crazy, scary, elusive, beautiful thing called life and the self. I had to find those sources of wisdom to learn how to thrive.

And since we can't connect with what's real about ourselves, we can't connect with what's real about anyone else. We fail to give and receive even half as much love as we could. We have to go all in and love ourselves so we can love others as well.

Yoga is often translated as "to yoke, to join, or to connect." The goal of yoga is connection: to our bodies, to our thoughts and feelings, to our spirits, to the sensations, causes, and consequences that come with the situations we face and the dramas we create. Yoga gave me the tools to experience all the facets of myself in both painful and pleasurable moments. And through discipline, I became able to observe, endure, nurture, challenge, embody, and trust what resides in my own consciousness — both the shadow and the light — without reacting or needing it to be different.

Now that I mentor people on body image, reframing their past and personal empowerment, I've seen clients get comfortable and real with themselves in many ways. Some dance naked in front of a mirror, wear a tiny bikini on the beach, or have sex with the lights on. For others, the milestones that mark peace with themselves will be less audacious, like the happiness felt when we wear a favorite dress or the day we feel as sexy in sweatpants and an old college T-shirt as we do in killer red heels.

To make peace with our emotions, some of us will share the stories of our experiences with large groups of people or a few close friends, and others will simply stop running away from feeling and allow themselves to sit with their emotions in the privacy of their home. One path to healing is not more superior than the other as long as we do it for the unconditional love of ourselves.

Exercises #4

1.) What are you struggling with?
2.) Take a moment and allow yourself to get really brave. Have you been holding yourself back in your process of growth, recovery, or healing?
3.) How can you deepen your process and take real responsibility and action from this moment forward?

Show Of Strength

Overcoming Samskaras

One of my most influential teachers, Jeffrey, always says what I need to hear at the exact right time. On one particular morning, I went to his yoga class excited to practice, but also concerned about the mountain of work I had to do and the many responsibilities that come with being a new mom and a new business owner. Taking three hours out of my day to practice at the studio where I started to take my yogic path seriously had become a rare occurrence.

"If you were standing next to a super powerful river without any rocks, you wouldn't realize the water's power," Jeffrey said during his lesson. "However, if you were to stand by another river of the same strength, and it had massive boulders in it where the water crashed, you would have no question about the river's power. Challenges don't make us stronger. They reveal the strength that we already have."

He was teaching us about how life's challenges show us our capabilities. I remember loving this wording because I always disliked the saying "obstacles make us stronger." When I'm facing a challenge and someone says this, I want to scream. The saying is in the same category as "no pain, no gain." It teaches us that punishing and hurting ourselves is only the way to get tough enough to handle life. This is the extreme philosophy I had as a professional dancer and perfectionist student that trapped me in a lifestyle of self-abuse. It took me a long time to realize that when we believe that struggle makes us stronger, we create ways to make hardship the cornerstone of our lives instead of gentleness and ease.

I've learned I don't need to beat myself up to become resilient. Growth and evolution naturally occur when I learn to approach problems from a different perspective. The power of my mind to learn from patterns of the past and take responsibility for my future is what makes me strong. My spirit is what powers me to keep trying no matter how many times I fail.

I've also learned that I'm not always going to come up against an obstacle and smoothly flow around it. Sometimes I'll crash and create white water in my life. There are usually a few rocks on my path. Some are buried deep inside me. Others are external. Often, the same obstacles impact so many people that they've become a part of our culture and society. These challenges can seem so insurmountable that it's easy to want to avoid them. Others keep popping up even after we're sure we've worked through them. Yoga philosophy calls these challenges *samskaras*.

Samskaras are imprints or impressions on the mind created from past experience that cause us to react to certain situations in the exact same ineffective way. When you come up against an issue again and again, that's usually a sign you're dealing with a samskara. These patterns make themselves most obvious when we're in pain, lots of it. We find ourselves having the same problems and disappointments with our new boyfriend as we did with the four that came before him. We find ourselves completely broke after making yet another promise to manage our money more carefully. Our *karma* has us stuck in a rut again and again.

Every time a samskara appears, we have the opportunity to either smooth out the impression or continue to carve its stronghold on our psyche, based on the way we respond. We can surrender to the fate of our previous conditioning or develop new neural pathways to create a destiny. Once we are aware of our patterns, habits, and tendencies, we have a choice to try something different. We can think and behave as we always have, or we can expand our perspective, nix the victim archetype, shift our actions, and break through the cycle of suffering.

The idea that we behave according to unique patterns we've been learning our whole lives is a simple concept to understand. Our behavior is hard to actually change, especially when we've never experienced life another way. Some samskaras will take a lifetime or much longer to clear, and others will dissolve in an instant when we see them clearly. However, once we become aware of patterns in our thinking and behaviors that lead to suffering for ourselves and others, it's our responsibility to do something different. If we truly want *moksha*, to liberate ourselves from the human condition, we must break free from what we know is keeping us stuck in pain and stagnation.

The physical practice of yoga asana offers us a way to observe our thoughts and actions, and release the patterns of the past by using the power of the mind to increase the strength and flexibility in our body. The limitations we experience in each pose are a metaphor for the samskaras we experience in everyday life. We overcome our internal obstacles as we break through barriers in each posture. Our bodies can teach us so much about the human potential if we allow ourselves to listen because our bodies are the vessel of our spirit.

I used to struggle like crazy in *sirsasana* (headstand pose). It was so hard for me for some reason. Regardless of my background as a dancer and my extensive knowledge of anatomy and movement, I could not do it. The more I tried, the worse it got.

I had to memorize two specific asana sequences to graduate Jivamukti teacher training. Both required me to hold headstand for five minutes. About halfway through the month long training, I still couldn't hold headstand on my own, but I always knew when it was getting close in the sequence. My thoughts would bounce between dreading it and psyching myself up to hold it well before it was time for the pose. I was never in the moment.

Even though I knew wholeheartedly that true yoga is not about asana — it's about the willingness to change — and that my self-worth shouldn't have anything to do with this posture, I allowed headstand to define me as a person, a yogi, and an aspiring teacher. One day, in a rare moment of balance as I got into headstand at practice, Jeffrey came by and grabbed my ankles.

He said, "Don't come down."

That was it.

"Don't come down."

I exasperatedly thought, "Seriously? You think it's that easy?"

And then I found out it was. I stayed up for the rest of the 50 breaths, totaling five minutes upside down.

Headstand continued to challenge me after that, but the struggle was different because I knew I could do it. It became a practice of getting out of my own way to find ease in the midst of difficulty, rather than battle with myself. It was like in *The Wizard of Oz* when Glinda says, "You always had the power, you just had to learn it for yourself."

Nothing changed about headstand. My relationship with headstand changed at the only moment it could. We unlock lessons when we are ready, often with the support of others. We overcome our samskaras one by one. The power to do so is part of our nature.

Exercise #5

1.) Where in you life have you noticed a pattern that is causing suffering in some way?
2.) What steps can you take today to start making a shift in your thinking and your actions?

.

Sadhana With Style

My Life-Changing Wardrobe Malfunction

In 2012, I accidentally gave away nearly my entire wardrobe. At the time, I was pregnant and moving into a house with my partner, Brian. I boxed up all of the clothes that didn't fit me at the time to put into storage, give to friends, and donate to the thrift store.

A few months after my son was born, I was ready again for my old wardrobe that I'd pieced together over many years of scouting out vintage shops, designer clearance racks, merch tables at live music events, and yoga and Pilates studios. My style was unique and intentional, part of my efforts to define myself on my own terms. I was proud of it. Maternity clothes didn't feel like me at all.

I was really excited when two large boxes came out of the attic. One was filled with super fancy dresses. As I opened the second box, full of worn out yoga practice clothes, it became clear. It was all gone — no nice yoga teaching clothes, no jeans, no cute tops, no casual dresses or fun skirts. I was shocked and sent out a tiny prayer that whoever found my clothes would love them.

The second *Noble Truth* in Buddhism is that all suffering is caused by attachment and aversion. Attachment and aversion are the human responses to another Noble Truth, impermanence. The nature of impermanence is not always a fun fact to accept. However, when we can, we grow to see there are opportunities to practice non-attachment and acceptance all of the time. There's usually a grieving process involved. But once you become comfortable with it, even the biggest blunders become entertaining. The art of losing becomes a form of *sadhana,* a disciplined ritual practice we take on to transcend our human egos.

This lesson was multilayered, as lessons usually are. On the surface, the message was obvious. I had to let go of my clothes and, with them, my grip on my belief that material things bring happiness. I never thought I was attached to stuff. I'd moved 22 times in the past 15 years, and with each move I practiced letting go of what no longer served me, keeping only what felt wonderful to have around. As people, places, and things disappear from our lives, we make space for something new to come in that better reflects the person we've become.

And yet I was attached to my style. I didn't realize it until all my clothes were gone. The truth was that I had to let go of more than those clothes. I needed to let go of some key parts of the person I had been because a new phase of my life had sprung. I had to make space in my closet, heart, and home for the expression of a new self: my partner self, mama self, entrepreneur self, and teacher self. My self-focused, independent, wild, and rebellious persona needed to, in some ways, go with the clothes.

The feeling of loss had little to do with my newfound dearth of vintage day dresses. It ultimately stemmed from the attachment I had to the parts of myself my clothes represented. I was changing forms. My roles were shifting in the lives of others. I now had another living being dependent on me for its survival and health. Yet I knew my wholeness had to exist in a place beyond all that because one day this form would change too.

Non-attachment is different than detachment. When we detach, we limit our connection to the highs and lows that help us evolve as we confront and harness the reality of impermanence. When we practice non-attachment, we are able to see ourselves and the events in our lives from an elevated perspective. We can notice the symbolism in the tough moments that arise. We see beyond black-and-white thinking to the vast array of options for how we can respond productively to a situation. We choose to use every change as fuel for growth, grist for the mill, an opportunity to make peace with the nature of life that humans don't get to decide. When the things we define ourselves as are stripped away — be it a phase in life or our favorite combat boots — we come to more deeply know our eternal selves.

Exercise #6

1.) Have you been using the external to define you in some way? Perhaps through your style, the music you like, the places you hang out, or the roles that you play?
2.) Who are you underneath it all?

Practical Magic

Manifesting Your Desires in the Real World

Manifesting isn't magic. There's a lot of talk in the New Age world about manifesting miracles and a fabulous, fulfilling life through positive thinking alone. And it's far more complicated than that. That's what I've found.

Yes, we are always manifesting our reality. If our mind is filled with weeds, we won't grow any flowers. That's why in *Yoga Sutra* II.23 it says, "When disturbed by bothersome thoughts, think the opposite."

Thoughts are the seeds for our actions. If we have negative thoughts about ourselves, we may never even try to do what we dream. It helps to replace negative thoughts with positive ones, but that's only part of the practice of manifestation. There are skilled actions we have to take. Learning how to manifest with intention is a lifelong process that requires patience.

When I first started my business, I took a premature leap of faith, thinking the universe would provide me with what I needed to survive if I followed my spiritual calling. I decided to quit all my yoga and Pilates teaching gigs to start coaching and mentoring at-risk populations and people working on mindfulness full time.

My intentions were benevolent. I was driven by my big wish to provide for my family while doing work that I 100 percent believed in with all my heart. I was ready to mentor individuals and groups of students, to write, and speak to audiences about the ancient teachings that had shifted my modern life in such miraculous ways. I was ready to pay it forward and pass along what I had spent a decade studying. After so much searching, I knew that coaching and teaching others about movement and healing and the nature of the mind was my life mission. It's my avocation. It's my purpose. Yet despite all my positive thinking, I couldn't make ends meet.

I asked for guidance and read business blogs geared toward spiritually minded creative people. I completed business courses and attended webinars. The messages were largely the same: set your intentions, visualize your ideal life every day, make a plan, let go of the plan, relax and trust that it will all come exactly as it should. So I did. And slowly, very slowly, a little bit of progress would happen, but not nearly enough to pay for my mortgage, my son's preschool tuition, and other living expenses.

There had to be some limiting internal belief that was keeping me stuck, I thought. Maybe somewhere deep inside I still didn't believe I was worth it. Maybe I spent so many years in my teens and twenties idealizing the bohemian lifestyle depicted in *Rent* that I programed myself to never be able to make a middle-class living.

But it wasn't that. It wasn't my beliefs about myself that were holding me back. It was my belief in instant manifestation. My business started gaining momentum when I stopped believing in magical thinking and began to embrace practical magic.

We make the leap into the world of practical magic by making sure that every intention, prayer, and affirmation is paired with practical, inspired actions every day. We don't add action to our to-do list. We make it our default way of being. With time, eventually results will bloom.

What is manifestation anyway? It's a way of saying that life is a creative process and we are all creators. We create ourselves. We create other people. We create the world of things. That's the gift of being human. We get to create a life that models our dreams.

To set an intention is to make a contract with yourself and the Universe, God, whatever you call the unifying, connective force larger than yourself, that you'll take action to become the kind of person you envision for the good of the collective. Vision and intention ultimately determine how we focus our actions, but no matter how much I dream or pray, I am the one who is going to make my visions a reality. There is no supernatural energy that will accomplish my goals for me like the marketing of New Age philosophy teaches us to believe. We can't will everything we want to happen on a timeline, either. We have to make moves, knowing there will be an equal and opposite reaction to all of our choices. We must step into flow and be open to all possibilities.

Those of us who are brave enough to follow our dreams and set intentions each day often do so to uplift ourselves, to feel positive and purposeful in a world that can cause us to become lost, violent, and negative if we aren't carefully cultivating a peaceful inner landscape. However, the lasting joy and bliss we seek does not usually come from attaining the actual thing, person, or circumstance we so desire at that moment. It's not about the rush of getting what we want when we want it. It's not about being an omnipotent person, capable of bending the world to our whims. Lasting confidence and success come from the deep knowing that we are on the right path, making progress, taking care of our responsibilities. We feel that life is working.

When we finally embody this state of well-being, the outward circumstances of our lives may look very different than we imagined. We may fall in love with an older man who is a carpenter instead of a young guitar player. We may find a home that we love in the green hills of Ireland instead of on a tropical island. To be truly free, we must take action and give up attachments without surrendering our divinely oriented sense of direction to empower ourselves and others.

My business finally began to flow and grow when I stopped trying to "make it happen" in one strict package. I had to let go of my do-or-die,

100 percent in-at-all-costs, happen-right-now mentality. I had to return to teaching Pilates in class settings so I could attract clients naturally without experiencing financial desperation. In doing so, I freed myself up to do the work that I love with love, rather than force and angst. I've learned that in the society we live in, doing what you love on exactly your own terms is a privilege obtained by those who have taken the time to build a solid foundation to support their work.

It's easy to want to believe we are all powerful creators. And the truth is we are. However, we can't manifest things like a career, a long-term relationship, or financial prosperity instantly. We have to hire financial advisors, lawyers, and virtual assistants. We have to keep a side job while we build our business. We have to study with a great teacher for years before we can ethically strike out on our own. We have to take the risk to have a difficult conversation with our partner to build an authentic connection. If we can't commit to the process, we'll never make it anywhere.

The recent cultural obsession with magical thinking is unconsciously based in fear and the avoidance of what's actually required to make something happen in reality. Magical thinking is a form of self-sabotage. Because when it doesn't work exactly the way we want it to, it confirms our self-image as a failure.

We build a strong platform to support our dreams step-by-step. *Pade pade.* When we rush or doubt the process, we rob ourselves of the opportunity to be present for the shifts that unfold when we use our heart and our head. Years later, I now look at my life and see all of my desires are coming to fruition — speaking, writing, teaching, mentoring — but they haven't happened at all in the way that I planned. That is the magic of manifesting.

Exercise #7

1.) Where in your life have you been relying on magical thinking?
2.) What can you do today to marry practicality, intention, and action to turn your magical thinking into practical magic?
3.) Where in your life are you relying too much on regimen, formality, and discipline?
4.) What can you do to realign your desires to spirit again?

The Truth Is One (& Two)

Building Intimacy

The truth is simple. Telling the truth is a little more complicated. Why? Because we always tell the truth from our own subjective perspective. Our truth is just that: ours. A select few of us may spend a lifetime seeking to understand universal truths. However, we are rarely the bearers of it.

You see, there is truth, and there is Truth. One comes from the self, and the other comes from that which is larger than ourselves. In every religion I know of, truth telling is a virtue. The ninth commandment says, "Thou shalt not bear false witness against his neighbor." What that means to me is we are meant to protect each other (and ourselves) through our speech. It's our duty to speak from the heart, to use our words to cultivate integrity while leaving space for people to share their perceptions. When we take a risk to tell our truth, we inevitably find that we are all different. The Truth is that we are also equal.

There are many ways to describe intimacy. One definition is that intimacy is being safe to share your reality with another person. When our experiences are treated as inferior by others, all potential for intimacy dies. Relationships quickly become a battle zone. And because of this, building intimacy is a spiritual practice that forces us to live and love in the reality of pluralism. In an intimate, healthy relationship, two separate people learn to act in a way creates a third entity: their bond and everything that two people, joined in love, can create with it.

To do this, we have to disarm our many defenses, all the impulses within us that want to run away, attack, or shut down when our feelings get spiked and painful memories arise. Humans interpret life through the eyes of the past, and because of this, old insecurities, childhood wounds, and recollections of all the times we weren't treated as an equal will surface when we let our guards down and let someone close to our heart. Relationships are a mirror onto which we project all the parts of ourselves that we don't want to see, because what is in one person exists in all people. When we commit to the path of health, authenticity, and evolution, it becomes our duty to fine-tune all the sides of ourselves that keep us from loving and standing beside others.

I used to carry so much pain and shame about my past that I couldn't share my story with another person, be it a romantic partner or a friend, without falling fast into painting myself as the victim. Doing so would instantly color our interactions in the same light and perpetuate the suffering from my past because I had taught my partner to see me as a victim and a martyr, even though I was working to see myself as strong, capable, and responsible for my own life experience.

When I met Brian, my partner in life and love, I was practicing staying in my integrity about my past in a way that didn't recreate old patterns. Being open, authentic, and raw is an interesting practice because it isn't always received well. Sometimes people really do freak out when we tell them about our shocking experiences. Our fears of being judged are realized. Still, it's worth it. Sometimes, and sometimes more often than we think, people surprise us. Our openness will signal that it's safe for them to reveal all the ways they've transformed themselves.

On our third or fourth date, I invited Brian to my house for dinner. I rarely cooked, so it was a big deal. The gravity of the night was enhanced by our conversation. I was totally open with him when discussing my past, and he was open with me. We had both recently had prior relationships end in traumatic ways, so connecting so deeply and honestly with another person was really scary. We were afraid the doom and despair would repeat. I remember being freezing cold and shaky even though I was eating warm, spicy soup. It's the feeling I have had many times since in moments of extreme personal growth and vulnerable soul connection.

Brian met me exactly where I was. He didn't react in any noteworthy way. It wasn't a magical movie moment. It was simple. The only drama was my own internal battle to rise up and be fully seen. Even though our pasts were different, our present was that moment and we were fully there together.

Our relationship has not been the princess story version of perfect, but it's perfect for us. It was unstable at first. The fear of intimacy and trusting another caused us to break up many times before we committed to be together in our journey as a couple and as parents to our son. Most of my friends thought that I was crazy for staying in the relationship. What they didn't see is that each breakup felt like a breakthrough rather than destruction or finality. We have always wanted each other to be the best possible version of ourselves. Sometimes we could do that growing together, and sometimes we needed to take different paths for awhile. However, once we dedicated ourselves to working toward true intimacy, we stopped letting our fears and defenses jerk us around.

Openly communicating in a way that is kind and loving to the other has become the keystone of our relationship. When I share my experiences with Brian, it's not about emotionally dumping or acting like he's responsible for my feelings or can make them go away. I don't speak to protect myself and hurt him. I've had to learn that how I express my truth makes all difference in determining if we get closer after conflict and misunderstandings or if we retreat to distance and protect ourselves from each other.

Patanjali — the wise sage who wrote the Sutras — gives us the direction of *ahimsa*, non-harming. It's important to share our side of a situation in a way that doesn't accuse the other person of being bad or express any other harsh statements that could damage someone's self-esteem. Even when we tell it like it is, we must always be mindful that although our truth is real, it is not the whole story. Everyone is fighting hard for the right to be here as the person they are.

This goes in every relationship — in both work and my personal life. I've found that the way I express my truth is 50 percent of the equation that will reveal if a relationship becomes stronger, if it implodes, or if I am forced to realize that while the other person may be valuable to me, they are not interested in my reality. I am not safe. It's time to either end the relationship or shift the way that person is in my life to a new position where they won't be able to repeatedly hurt me in the same way.

Conflict is bound to arise. I can't avoid it, and I also can't win if I want the other person to lose, because creating a win-lose situation won't deepen our connection. I have to move beyond the solipsism of my own ego and all the ways it seems I've been wronged, to treat another person's point of view as equal. Humbling myself to this process always results in a miraculous shift in my awareness. When I take a risk and am met by the other person, there is always more love on the other end than when I began.

When we take a moment to pause and check in with the real objective of communication —and that is connection — we can stop ourselves from resorting to the 25 or so defense mechanisms humans would be far better functional without and, instead, open up, let down our guard, and use the conversation as an opportunity to increase honesty, trust, and understanding. Conflict can teach us to honor feelings, advocate for our safety, and change our behaviors to show others they are respected. It takes two people capable of this process to keep a healthy relationship intact. Authentic relationships are not for the faint of heart. They are, however, what make life worth living.

Exercises #8

If you struggle with conflict, ask yourself:

1.) Do you want peace, or do you want to be right?
2.) Do you want love, or do you want power?

Wisdom From The Southern Yoda

The Universe Provides

I once met a guy on the beach in a random, magical encounter. On Wednesday evenings, I teach a yoga class at the Sixth Street west block on Folly Beach. Usually, it's a full, fun class. On this particular night, nobody came. I interpreted this as a sign that I needed to take time for myself to play and rest because sometimes we get what we need by not getting anything.

I decided to walk to the other side of the beach, right across from the little yellow cottage I used to call home. I noticed an older guy with long, curly blond hair and a fluffy salt-and-pepper beard. He was wearing board shorts, nonchalantly riding his bike in my direction with a huge smile on his face. We got to the steps where the beach meets the road at the same time and said hello. I had my yoga mat, a Hula-Hoop, and a brand new journal in my hands.

"You appear all set to have an awesome evening," he said.

"It looks like you already are!" I responded.

As we walked toward the beach, he told me about his experience teaching yoga for 15 years and how amazing it is to live on Folly Beach and watch it evolve. He was full of stories of all the times he asked the universe to provide something for him and how his requests were always answered. The right people appear at the right time. He finds the perfect object for his house while walking around the island. The right piece of property is for sale exactly when he is looking to buy. He said he was always so certain everything he needed would be taken care of by life.

"I know that's true," I told him. "I've had experiences when it's been proven many times, but I still struggle with trust. I should have faith all the time instead of most of the time."

He said, "Don't say should. No shoulds allowed. Just be ready." Then he walked away into the waves.

Apparently, I'd just ran into the Southern hippie version of Yoda.

As he was bodysurfing, I laid down my mat and started to write. I wrote a massive list of thank-yous. Thank you for my partner. Thank you for my son. Thank you for my ability to make a living doing work that I love. Thank you for the sun that felt amazing and was lighting up the sky in a hazy pink glow as it went down. Thank you. I filled many pages, acknowledging the blessings in my life that are easy to take for granted.

Then I made a list of everything I was ready for. I am ready to go all in and create an amazing course for my students. I am ready to write this book. I am ready to travel. I am ready to surf again. I am ready to consistently have enough cash in the bank to easily live the lifestyle I love.

I tapped into really feeling gratitude for all that I had and worked to achieve. I opened myself to the possibility that I could call into my life all that I desired. I knew I couldn't wish it into existence, but I could let go of any doubts that it would come and get ready to receive.

When we say we want something but on some level believe we don't deserve it or are unprepared in some way to create or receive it, we send mixed signals to our creative power and the creative flow of the universe. Mixed signals yield mixed results. When our dreams aren't realized, we begin to believe they can't be. When we shift our thinking, get out of our own way to see all that we've cultivated thus far, and ask for what we want while deeply believing we deserve it, we create massive shifts in how we experience life. All of a sudden, the goodness and abundance that was previously invisible or taken for granted builds with momentum as life presents us with more and more. But we must be ready to go. When we know what we want, we can't wait until the time is right to truly dive in.

I am ready!

I am ready.

I finished writing as "Southern Hippie Yoda" finished his swim. He left the beach. I started my yoga asana practice — and on that day it was fluid and easy. No long holding. Nothing rushed. I decided I was ready to try pinchamayurasana (forearm stand), which I had been avoiding for months. I was done worrying about my shoulder, which was still tight from holding my son when he was a baby and typing so much every day. I wanted to move.

I calmly floated into the posture. I repeated the silent mantra "I am ready" in my mind. I somersaulted out, and that was that. No big deal. No pain. No fear. So I did it many more times. I realized the only thing that had been holding me back was my own belief that I wasn't ready.

So "I am ready" became a mantra of sorts that guided me to take my life to a new level. I declared it and I became it. If I didn't receive what I expected or wanted, I knew it was because I wasn't ready.

Prayers are answered as they are answered. The practice is to open ourselves up to receive in Divine time and to thank the universe for all the little signs that prepare us for what's to come. To live with purpose, we must be willing to surrender our personal will for that of something larger. Whenever I'm losing faith, I remember one of my favorite prayers:

"Make me an instrument for Thy will; not mine but Thine be done; free me from anger, jealousy and fear; fill my heart with joy and compassion. Shanti. Shanti. Shanti. Hari Om."

The second we let go, we begin to let the universe do its work.

Exercise #9

1.) What are you ready for?

Life On Purpose

You are the Message

"Your life is the most perfect memorial," said the priest at my grandma's funeral. In his eulogy, he spoke about how we could bring the essence of my grandmother's spirit into our lives to keep her alive on Earth. She was a woman of incredible faith. She steadfastly supported those she loved.

It was an excellent call to action. For to love and appreciate qualities in another without adopting them ourselves is to miss the point. Knowing is not enough. Taking action is paramount.

David Life says that he views all of his students as angels, capable of anything. He sees us as people with unlimited potential. I also deeply believe this is true. When I see the good in others, it's an opportunity for me to rise. The goodness in them can be the goodness in me too.

The people who change the world and become known for it are no different than those who positively impact the lives of just a few. The inspiration and intention comes from the same place. Their positive actions and dedication to live by a moral code ripples out into the world in the same way.

There's a parable about a man who walks down a beach and throws starfish back into the ocean so they don't dry out in the sun and die. His friend tells him, "It's useless. You can't possibly save them all, so why does it matter? What difference does it make?"

The man throws another starfish back into the water and says, "It makes a difference for this one."

We often hold ourselves back from stepping into our full potential as beings of light because the concept of what that would look like feels too vast to even fathom how to go about taking the actual steps. I see my teachers and idols as being so loving, authentic, kind, smart, sophisticated, and all the other things I admire. I forget I can be all those qualities too. In fact, I already am.

There is a phrase from the Kundalini tradition — *sat nam*. It means I am. We all have the same essence of light that is our true identity.

If you ask yourself the question "Who am I?", you are bound to find many answers. We are a collection of the pieces of our personality, our behaviors and life experiences, and we are more than that. We have within us a spark of the Divine, the *Atman*. We are not separate from God, the energy of the Universe, or whatever label you define that which is inexplicable by linear thought but far greater than traditional notions of the self. We just forget. When we reclaim that spark within us, even for an instant, we tap into our limitlessness, our potential. When we can't feel the presence of the divine after making initial contact, we practice leaning into faith. We remember that even when we can't see the spark within us, it's there, ready for us to reclaim at any given time.

The people in this world who seem to move mountains live in a different way. They do the hard work of sharpening their conscious awareness to see the ways they perpetuate the problems humanity faces, and they experiment on how to be part of the solution. They share the light within them by acting as guardians of life, agents of peace and social change. They accomplish this by being mindful in their every foot step. They work on themselves every day.

The people I have met who are creating massive change in the world are also some of the most humble. They credit teachers and teachings, the instruments of the Atman, for their actions. They let go of the negative beliefs about their false selves that kept them from doing great work in the world so the light within can fully shine.

Ego, what we are taught to identify ourselves by, can't accomplish this. Ego prioritizes our own needs and desires no matter how they impact others. Ego martyrs us because of the painful situations we've been subject to until we are left depleted, jaded, and have nothing to give. Connection with the part of ourselves that is perfect, whole, timeless, unlimitedly capable, and the same as everything else in the cosmos is what allows us to walk in the world of ego with peace and love.

We each contribute to the suffering present on the planet. It's the nature of karma, the reslut of intention. It's part of our programming, our animal nature. Many ancient spiritual texts say that our purpose in this world is to liberate ourselves and assist others along their path. But to become the kind of person who walks along the beach saving starfish, to be on the path of a *Bodhisattva*, we must undergo an experience of awakening to the impact of our decisions and our divine potential.

According to multiple spiritual traditions, it takes lifetimes to actualize the perfect love within you in the world. You have to call yourself out if you're falling off the path. You have to be a warrior, committed to finding balance between lightness and darkness in every moment. And at your last breath, the sum total of your actions creates your legacy, your imprint on life.

How will people remember you?

What is the imprint you'll leave on the world?

What will people say at your memorial?

It helps to remember that we have a choice in all of this all of the time. We are not helpless. Everyone encounters people that show us the worst of human behavior — and of course we don't want to be anything like them. Of course we want to think of ourselves as better than that. However, we forget that we've hurt people too, perhaps not in the same exact way, but in some way that left them with similar damage and feelings of emotional pain.

Rather than place judgement on others and ourselves as good or bad, we can work on mastering the sides of ourselves they've shown us. We can choose to exude the qualities they couldn't offer. We can give what is missing from our lives and the world to others. We can be the change. Our lives can commemorate the kindness others have offered us. Through our thoughts, words, and actions, we pay it forward. We find our purpose by living on purpose.

Index

1. Ahimsa - nonharming; restraining you behavior toward others in such a way that you do not cause harm to them with your thoughts, words, or deeds; the first yama from Patanjali's Ashtanga system. Ahimsa is the touchstone of all yogic practices.

2. Arjuna - a hero prince in the Bhagavad Gitahe.

3. Atman - the Divine Self, the indwelling soul; that which identifies absolute Brahman rather than the limited form of body and mind.

4. Bhavantu - bhav + antu. Bhav - the Divine mood or state of unified existence. Antu - may it be so; antu used at the end of a mantra turns the statement into a powerful pledge.

5. The Bhagavad Gita - translation: *The Song of the Lord*. Written circa 200 BC, it is an episode from the epic Mahabharata composed by the sage Vyasa. Considered an essential reference book for the practice of yoga.

6. Bodhisattva - a Buddhist term used to describe one who has attained Nirvana, enlightenment. One who has realized the True nature of Self and vows out of compassion to live among the unenlightened to assist them in their journey toward realization.

7. Buddhism - Buddhism is a living tradition, passed from teacher to student, as a set of pragmatic instructions and techniques for cultivating sanity and brilliance in ourselves and our world. Its ancient wisdom is as relevant and useful today as over the centuries of its long history.

8. Dharma - (1) Destiny. (2) In Buddhism, Dharma is the essential Truth, or the doctrine or teachings of the Buddha. (3) Law of the Universe in which the essential nature of the individual is that of the cosmos.

9. Dharma Yuddha - righteous Warfare, such as the battle in the Mahabharata in which Arjuna is going to battle and listening to the teachings of Krishna.

10. The Gita - the Bhagavad Gita.

11. Gunas - the qualities that make up the manifest world of Mother Nature. Sattva (lightness), Raja (activity), Tamas (inertia).

12. Guru - the remover of darkness, the teacher.

13. Hari - the remover (As in Hari Om, a powerful mantra to remove suffering.)

14. Jivamukti Yoga - lineage of yoga cofounded by Sharon Gannon and David Life. Described as a path to enlightenment through compassion. The Jivamukti Yoga method consists of Ahimsa (non-violence), Bhakti (devotion), Dhyana (meditation), Nada (deep listening), and Shastra (study of ancient teachings).

15. Karma - from the Sanskrit root word ker, which means action. Any thought, word, or deed. The Law of Karma is the law of cause and effect based in intention.

16. Karuna - the Buddhist concept of compassion.

17. Krishna - "the one who attracts" beloved Hindu God, avatar of Lord Vishnu.

18. Lokah - location, realm, all universes existing now

19. Mahabharata - one of two major Sanskrit epics of ancient India, which includes the Bhagavad Gita.

20. Maitri - friendliness, loving kindness, metta.

21. Mantra - (1) a word or sound repeated to aid meditation. (2) a Vedic hymn. (3) a statement or slogan repeated frequently.

22. The Middle Path - a way of being described in Buddhist teachings that is between two extremes, one of sense pleasures and one of self-modification.

23. Moksha - liberation

24. Mudita - pure joy unadulterated by self-interest.

25. New Age - a broad movement characterized by alternative approaches to traditional Western culture, with an interest in spirituality, mysticism, holism, and environmentalism.

26. Nia - the art of movement the body's way. A cardio-dance workout, a movement practice, and lifestyle based on the intelligent design of the body.

27. Noble Truth - the truths of noble oneness that express the orientation of Buddhism.

28. Om - the sound symbol of God (Pranavah); the most powerful mantra, the primal sound, the Nadam

29. Pade pade - step-by-step.

30. Patanjali - there is a disagreement about when he lived, with speculations ranging from 3000 BC to 300 BC. He compiled the Yoga Sutras and is considered the founder of Yoga philosophy.

31. Pincha mayurasana - forearm stand, feathered peacock pose

32. Rajas - passion, dynamic activity, movement outward, external creativity, one of the three gunas.

33. Sadhana - conscious spiritual practice.

34. Samastah - all beings sharing the same location.

35. Samskaras - grooves or impressions that are etched onto the covering of a soul by every karma or action taken.

36. Sanskrit - the ancient language of India, a potent vibrational language with the inherent power to invoke what is spoken.

37. Sat nam - Sat + Nam, Sat = true, everlasting. Nam = name. This phrase likely comes from the teacher Gurmukh of the Kundalini tradition.

38. Satsang - Sat + anga. Sat = truth. Anga = attachment or limb. Association with those who remind you of your True potential. Community.

39. Satsang Charleston - a yoga shala, school for the study of yoga in Charleston, South Carolina.

40. Sattva - balance, lightness, purity, movement toward the inner, one of the three gunas.

41. Sattvic - having the qualities of the sattva.

42. Shanti - peace.

43. Sirsasana - headstand pose.

44. Sukhino - sweetness, centered in happiness and joy, free from suffering.

45. Svaha - may it be so.

46. Tamas - inertia, heaviness, darkness, obstinacy, stubbornness, one of the three gunas or qualities inherent in maya, the illusory world.

47. Upekshanam - acceptance, equanimity, indifference, disregard, neutrality.

48. Yoga - from yuj, to yoke; the yoking of the individual sense of self to the cosmic eternal Self; union with God, samadhi.

49. Yoga asana - the physical practice or exercises of yoga.

50. Yoga Shala - a school of the study of yoga teachings and practices.

51. The Yoga Sutra - scriptural source for the philosophical and practical system of yoga. Compiled by the sage Patanjali, composed of short terse statements (sutra), divided into four chapters dealing with samadhi (superconsciousness), sadhana (practice), siddhis (powers), and kaivalya (final enlightenment).

* Index definitions sourced from Jivamukti Yoga, notes taken over the course of many lectures with many teachers, and from Google and various dictionaries.

Gratitude

To my brilliant editor, Alison Sher: Thank you for pushing me to grow in a million ways and for being with me, in the arena, every step of the way. To Brian and Isaac: Thank you for every minute of every day. Walking beside you on this journey of life is magical and I am grateful every day. I love you guys. Thank you for being on my team. To my parents and my brother: "There ain't no mountain high enough..." Thanks and love, for it all. To Jessie Parks: Thank you for your skillful line edits. To Katy Quinn, Caryn Antos O'Hara, Brian Hoke, Megan Dupont, Michael Reynolds, and Audra Rhodes: Thank you for being the first readers. To Manorama, Brandt, Jules, Caryn, and Melanie: Thank you for taking the time to read this book and to offer your beautiful endorsements. I am deeply grateful. To Noah: Thank you from the bottom of my heart for your words. If this book can do for one person what Dharma Punx did for me, my heart will overflow with joy. To all of my teachers: Thank you for sharing your knowledge and believing in me. Special thanks to Polly, Jeffrey, and Andrea. To all of my students: Thank you for asking me to teach. It is an honor. I do not take the responsibility lightly. To all of my friends and family: Thank you for being a part of my story and allowing me to be a part of yours. To all of the readers: Thank you, thank you, thank you. Love. Love. Love.

Final Note To The Reader

Thank you for reading. I would love to stay connected and hear about your journey of living your life on purpose. I welcome comments and questions, and am happy to hold space for you and to be of service as best as possible.

You can find me at my website www.katieashley.org and on Instagram @katieashleylove

Much love,

Katie

Made in the USA
Middletown, DE
12 March 2022

62421175R00066